Journal Your Way To
SIGNIFICANCE

Find Purpose
When All You Feel Is Worthless

MATT PAVLIK

BRINGING YOUR
POTENTIAL
TO LIGHT

Christian Concepts
Centerville, Ohio

JOURNAL YOUR WAY TO SIGNIFICANCE
Copyright © 2020 by Matt Pavlik.

All rights reserved. No part of this book may be used or reproduced in any manner whatsoever without written permission except in the case of brief quotations embodied in critical articles or reviews.

Published in the United States of America by Christian Concepts (christianconcepts.com), an imprint of New Reflections Counseling, Inc. (newreflectionscounseling.com).

Although the author is a professional counselor, this book is not intended to be a replacement for professional counseling.

First Edition: June 2020

REL012150 RELIGION / Christian Living / Devotional Journal

Pavlik, Matthew Edward, 1971-
Journal Your Way To Significance / Matt Pavlik.

ISBN: 978-1-951866-02-0 (softcover)

1. Spiritual journals—Authorship—Religious aspects—Christianity
2. Diaries—Authorship—Religious aspects—Christianity

Journaling, Significance, Healing, Growth, Self-acceptance, Meaning (Philosophy), Rejection (Psychology), Self-deception

Scripture quotations marked NLT are taken from the Holy Bible, New Living Translation, copyright © 1996, 2004, 2015 by Tyndale House Foundation. Used by permission of Tyndale House Publishers, Inc., Carol Stream, Illinois 60188. All rights reserved.

Scripture quotations marked (NIV) are taken from the Holy Bible, New International Version®, NIV®. Copyright © 1973, 1978, 1984, 2011 by Biblica, Inc.™ Used by permission of Zondervan. All rights reserved worldwide. www.zondervan.comThe "NIV" and "New International Version" are trademarks registered in the United States Patent and Trademark Office by Biblica, Inc.™

Scripture quotations marked ESV are from the ESV® Bible (The Holy Bible, English Standard Version®), copyright © 2001 by Crossway Bibles, a publishing ministry of Good News Publishers. Used by permission. All rights reserved.

Scripture quotations marked TPT are from The Passion Translation®. Copyright © 2017, 2018 by Passion & Fire Ministries, Inc. Used by permission. All rights reserved. ThePassionTranslation.com.

Amplified Bible (AMP) Copyright © 1954, 1958, 1962, 1964, 1965, 1987 by The Lockman Foundation, La Habra, CA. All rights reserved. Used by Permission.

Scripture quotations marked (CEV) are from the Contemporary English Version Copyright © 1991, 1992, 1995 by American Bible Society, Used by Permission.

IMAGES

Truth #01: pixabay - freestocks-photos: 2942847
Truth #02: pixabay - fsHH: 2249111
Truth #03: pixabay - marvelmozhko: 2935722
Truth #04: pixabay - kimboda: 2901376
Truth #05: pxhere - 1171799
Truth #06: pixabay - geralt: 2775273
Truth #07: pexels - Plenio: 1118874
Truth #08: pixabay - azboomer: 790815
Truth #09: pixabay - AdinaVoicu: 1521943
Truth #10: pixabay - Free-Photos: 1246043
Truth #11: pixabay - SvetlozarHristov: 4797497
Truth #12: pixabay - geralt: 3169693
Truth #13: pexels - Piacquadio: 3853254
Truth #14: pxhere - rawpixel: 1434339
Truth #15: pxhere - 704019
Truth #16: unsplash - Walker: _-SwhhV7tSo
Truth #17: pxHere - 638522
Truth #18: pixabay - Tumisu: 4886221
Truth #19: pixabay - ErikSmit: 2706937
Truth #20: pxhere - 859191
Truth #21: pexels - Piacquadio: 3764011
Truth #22: pxhere - 1413913
Truth #23: pxhere - 1412493
Truth #24: pixabay - Free-Photos: 1209740
Truth #25: pixabay - Maryam62: 447233
Truth #26: pixabay - natureworks: 796788
Truth #27: pixabay - MarCuesBo: 3226408
Truth #28: pixabay - 272447: 987972
Truth #29: pixabay - cocoparisienne: 704357
Truth #30: pixabay - oliver-eyth: 943797

CONTENTS

Introduction: You Are Significant 1
Truth #01: God Made You In His Image 4
Truth #02: God Defines Your Worth 8
Truth #03: God Made You On Purpose 12
Truth #04: God Is Making You Look Like Christ 16
Truth #05: God Gives You Authority To Act On His Behalf 20
Truth #06: You Are A Target 24
Truth #07: You Can Overcome Fear 28
Truth #08: God Uses Truth To Strengthen You 32
Truth #09: God Uses Evil To Strengthen You 36
Truth #10: God Equips You With Power 40
Truth #11: You Are Savory 44
Truth #12: You Are Bright 48
Truth #13: You Are Gifted 52
Truth #14: You Are Needed 56
Truth #15: You Are Unique 60
Truth #16: You Are Enough 64
Truth #17: You Are More Important Than Your Popularity 68
Truth #18: You Are More Important Than Your Possessions 72
Truth #19: You Are More Important Than Your Performance 76
Truth #20: You Are More Important Than Your Pride 80
Truth #21: Your Faith Nourishes Your Self-Worth 84
Truth #22: God Made You For Peace And Contentment 88
Truth #23: God Made You To Experience Abundant Life Forever 92
Truth #24: Your Words Are Meaningful 96
Truth #25: Your Actions Are Meaningful 100
Truth #26: You Have A Destiny To Fulfill 104
Truth #27: You Are Unstoppable 108
Truth #28: Death Is A Doorway 112
Truth #29: Your Sacrifice Is Substantial 116
Truth #30: You Have A Mission To Fulfill 120

Introduction

You Are Significant

There once was a king who ruled all the people in the entire world. He generously offered a special blessing to those who visited him at his palace. Some people traveled to receive it, while others held only bitterness in their hearts for the king.

There was a woman who struggled with feeling useless and unimportant. She had one nagging thought that robbed her of the desire to receive the blessing. Also, she felt nervous about the whole idea of approaching the king. However, her need quickly drove her to the decision to visit the king.

Much to her suprise, she didn't have to wait long to see the king. She felt like she needed more time to practice what she wanted to say. She didn't want to be rude, but she also couldn't ask for a blessing she felt might be tainted or worthless. Yet here she was standing before the king of everyone.

"Oh King, I understand that you would freely bless any of your subjects who ask for it. If your blessing makes all of us special, meaning 'better' or 'greater', then wouldn't that make none of us special? How can you say that you value everyone, let alone me?"

The wise king looked upon the woman with understanding and compassion.

"You can be special to me without having a value that is greater than another. Such comparisons are born out of the low value you place on yourself. The value I assign each person is between that person and I. No one else needs to know or care what value I place on you. Out of their bitterness they may judge and assign a value, but it will be meaningless."

"I see, Oh King. May I ask what value you place on me?"

"True freedom is to receive the value I place upon you. You are priceless. I make no duplicates. I need you for a specific kingdom purpose that no one else can accomplish."

The woman's face brightened as she received the gift of the king's words. She thanked him and left to return home.

The king always made his visitors his highest priority. As each vistor felt and revealed an aching question on their heart, the king shared just the right insight they needed to see clearly. And that is exactly how the king bestowed a blessing on all who visited him. No further blessing could exceed it.

You're Valuable Because God Says You Are

God's perspective is the only one than can correctly determine your worth. Your life exeriences will easily influence your self-worth, often negatively. What you feel is permanent damage to your self-worth, God sees as some dirt that will wash off with a decisive cleansing. Underneath the muck, God is refurbishing you with the strength of His image.

So when Peter saw [John], he asked Jesus, "What's going to happen to him?" Jesus replied, "If I decide to let him live until I return, what concern is that of yours? You must still keep on following me!" So the rumor started to circulate among the believers that this disciple wasn't going to die. But Jesus never said that, he only said, "If I let him live until I return, what concern is that of yours?"
—John 21:21-23 TPT

Therefore, don't compare yourself to your brother or sister. You are significant enough by being you and following the plan Jesus has for you.

How To Use This Book

You'll gain more from your journaling experience when you journal in layers. Journaling in layers has four steps:
1. **Represent**: communicate what is internal or subconscious by expressing it in some external or explicit medium (words, symbols, sculptures).
2. **Rest**: acknowledge what you expressed, then wait. Let it simmer, percolate, steep. Focus on something else.
3. **Review**: revisit what you expressed, taking it back in and looking for understanding and meaning.
4. **Repeat**: return to step 1.

This book has 30 truth lessons. Respond to each truth, then return at a regular interval (1 day, 1 week, or 1 month) to reflect on the truth again, including all of your previous responses. Then, write a new response. This will deepen the truth for you.

If you want more details about this method, grab a free copy of *Journal In Layers So You Can Soar Like Eagles* at ChristianConcepts.com. It's a short read and it will help you gain more from your journaling.

God Made You In His Image

Then God said, "Let us make man in our image, after our likeness." So God created man in his own image, in the image of God he created him; male and female he created them.

—Genesis 1:26–27 ESV

Behold, children are a heritage from the Lord, the fruit of the womb a reward. Like arrows in the hand of a warrior are the children of one's youth. Blessed is the man who fills his quiver with them!

—Psalm 127:3-5 ESV

MATT PAVLIK

The moment someone chooses to trust in Jesus Christ, his sins are wiped away, and he is adopted into God's family. That individual is set apart as a child of God, with a sacred purpose.
—Charles Stanley

And because we are his children, God has sent the Spirit of his Son into our hearts, prompting us to call out, "Abba, Father." Now you are no longer a slave but God's own child. And since you are his child, God has made you his heir.
—Galatians 4:6-7 NLT

Journal Your Way to Significance

Because God made you uniquely in His image, you have incredible value. You share many of God's attributes like a child shares his parent's attributes. Before your parents conceived you, you existed as an idea in God's mind.

You are more like God than any other non-human creation. He gave you a heart capable of being open to Him. Sharing so much of the same design allows you to more deeply understand each other. God communicates with you using an inner language of love and care.

You share your humanity with Jesus. You can rule, love, and sacrifice just like He can. God is sending you, His child, into the world to complete a specific mission. You have a sacred purpose to glorify God in a way only you can do.

God Defines Your Worth

What do you think? If a man has a hundred sheep, and one of them has gone astray, does he not leave the ninety-nine on the mountains and go in search of the one that went astray?

—Matthew 18:12 ESV

Are not two sparrows sold for a penny? And not one of them will fall to the ground apart from your Father. But even the hairs of your head are all numbered. Fear not, therefore; you are of more value than many sparrows.

—Matthew 10:29–31 ESV

MATT PAVLIK

We suffer much agony because we try to get from people what only God can give us, which is a sense of worth and value. Look to God for what you need, not to people.

—Joyce Meyer

Christ died for us at a time when we were helpless and sinful. No one is really willing to die for an honest person, though someone might be willing to die for a truly good person. But God showed how much he loved us by having Christ die for us, even though we were sinful.

—Romans 5:6-8 CEV

Journal Your Way to Significance

God alone has the authority to determine your worth. His love makes you significant. God placed a value on you when He created you and when He died for you. He made you for a heavenly world, so you must look to it to see your true value.

God knows all the intimate details about you from your physical appearance to your daily circumstances. He says you are priceless even before you accomplish anything. Rejection from others might hurt, but it doesn't ultimately matter. Your disappointment and difficulties never diminish your worth.

God proves He values you by pursuing you, even if you run away from Him. Ask God to bestow upon you the blessing of your value. Believe He has a special relationship with you, then look to Him to experience your true worth.

God Made You On Purpose

For you created my inmost being; you knit me together in my mother's womb. I praise you because I am fearfully and wonderfully made; your works are wonderful, I know that full well.

—Psalm 139:13–14 NIV

And he made from one man every nation of mankind to live on all the face of the earth, having determined allotted periods and the boundaries of their dwelling place.

—Acts 17:26 ESV

MATT PAVLIK

Spiritual formation is for everyone. Just as there is an 'outer you' that is being formed and shaped all the time, like it or not, by accident or on purpose, so there is an 'inner you.' You have a spirit. And it's constantly being shaped and tugged at: by what you hear and watch and say and read and think and experience.
—John Ortberg

Therefore, if anyone is in Christ, he is a new creation. The old has passed away; behold, the new has come.
—2 Corinthians 5:17 ESV

Journal Your Way to Significance

Your self-image, how positively or negatively you view yourself, can change, but your God-given identity is permanent and unchanging. Who you are becoming isn't a moving target. God knows exactly who you are. There are no coincidences with God—everything that happens is significant.

You have a new, spiritual you with a new heart. God is like a farmer who plants a one of a kind seed. He nurtures you and helps you grow. Spiritual growth means your spirit is growing to better know and understand God.

You don't have to worry about who you're supposed to be. God has already taken care of that. You are as significant today as you were the day you were born. Ask God to open your eyes to the truth of how amazing you are.

Truth #04

God Is Making You Look Like Christ

The Lord and the Spirit are one and the same, and the Lord's Spirit sets us free. So our faces are not covered. They show the bright glory of the Lord, as the Lord's Spirit makes us more and more like our glorious Lord.

—2 Corinthians 3:17-18 CEV

Every branch in me that does not bear fruit he takes away, and every branch that does bear fruit he prunes, that it may bear more fruit.

—John 15:2 ESV

Within each of us exists the image of God, however disfigured and corrupted by sin it may presently be. God is able to recover this image through grace as we are conformed to Christ.

—Alister McGrath

For those God foreknew he also predestined to be conformed to the image of his Son, that he might be the firstborn among many brothers and sisters. And those he predestined, he also called; those he called, he also justified; those he justified, he also glorified.

—Romans 8:29-30 NIV

Journal Your Way to Significance

God is investing in you to restore you to the image of Christ. He meticulously shapes you to fit with His overall plans, which go beyond what you can imagine. To grow, you must cooperate with God as He recovers His image in you.

Spiritual growth happens as you become more of who He made you to be and less of who you aren't supposed to be. Jesus supplies you with all you need so you can bear fruit. You are becoming more gifted, capable, and loving.

Growth also happens as God removes sinful patterns in your life. To make you perfect like Christ, He prunes what doesn't fit with His image. Your new growth more than makes up for your loss. Tell God you want to experience joy while He restores you to your best form.

Truth #05

God Gives You Authority To Act On His Behalf

Then God said, "Let us make man in our image, after our likeness. And let them have dominion over the fish of the sea and over the birds of the heavens and over the livestock and over all the earth and over every creeping thing that creeps on the earth." And God blessed them. And God said to them, "Be fruitful and multiply and fill the earth and subdue it, and have dominion over the fish of the sea and over the birds of the heavens and over every living thing that moves on the earth."
—Genesis 1:26, 28 ESV

We are human, but we don't wage war as humans do. We use God's mighty weapons, not worldly weapons, to knock down the strongholds of human reasoning and to destroy false arguments. We destroy every proud obstacle that keeps people from knowing God. We capture their rebellious thoughts and teach them to obey Christ.
—2 Corinthians 10:3-5 NLT

Without God, life has no purpose, and without purpose, life has no meaning. Without meaning, life has no significance or hope. If you're alive, there's a purpose for your life.
—Rick Warren

Again, the Kingdom of Heaven can be illustrated by the story of a man going on a long trip. He called together his servants and entrusted his money to them while he was gone. He gave five bags of silver to one, two bags of silver to another, and one bag of silver to the last—dividing it in proportion to their abilities. He then left on his trip.
—Matthew 25:14-15 NLT

Journal Your Way to Significance

God entrusts you with great power and responsibility. He intends for you to make a significant contribution for the good of all so He puts precious resources in your care. What you do with your abilities affects the balance between good and evil.

God's Spirit plus your identity is an unstoppable authority. As you trust in God and make His truth your foundation, you can act boldly. Use all the power of God's truth to expose the enemy's false promises and illusions of hope.

God invests in you because He desires to see you bear fruit. You can trust He has given you good gifts that will accomplish His purposes. Don't withhold any of your abilities as you serve Him. When you are determined to honor God and you commit your efforts to Him, your plans will succeed.

Truth #06

You Are A Target

Remember how I told you that servants are not greater than their master. So if people mistreat me, they will mistreat you. If they do what I say, they will do what you say.

—John 15:20 CEV

You know how badly we had been treated at Philippi just before we came to you and how much we suffered there. Yet our God gave us the courage to declare his Good News to you boldly, in spite of great opposition.

—1 Thessalonians 2:2 NLT

MATT PAVLIK

Spiritual warfare makes us think of demon possession, horrific demonstrations of satanic control, and dramatic exorcisms. But Scripture presents spiritual warfare not as the violent, bizarre end of the Christian life, but as what the Christian life is!
—Paul David Tripp

Be on your guard and stay awake. Your enemy, the devil, is like a roaring lion, sneaking around to find someone to attack.
—1 Peter 5:8 CEV

God has no weakness within Himself, so the enemy can't defeat Him. However, the enemy can hurt God by hurting you. You wouldn't be facing opposition if you weren't important.

The devil hates who you are because you have God's Spirit of love and power within you. He will attack you where you most uniquely represent God, and that's exactly where you'll feel the most intense rejection.

The devil's lies are his attempt to demoralize you and make you believe you are worthless. Don't believe him. God gives you courage amidst opposition to complete your mission to declare His truth. Stay vigilant with your God-given authority. Stand strong against the enemy who wants to destroy you. Remember who you are, and whose you are.

Truth #07

You Can Overcome Fear

And I will give you a new heart, and a new spirit I will put within you. And I will remove the heart of stone from your flesh and give you a heart of flesh.

—Ezekiel 36:26 ESV

For everyone who has been born of God overcomes the world. And this is the victory that has overcome the world—our faith.

—1 John 5:4 ESV

MATT PAVLIK

Where does your security lie? Is God your refuge, your hiding place, your stronghold, your shepherd, your counselor, your friend, your redeemer, your savior, your guide? If He is, you don't need to search any further for security.

—Elisabeth Elliot

*You will keep in perfect peace
all who trust in you,
all whose thoughts are fixed on you!
Trust in the LORD always,
for the LORD GOD is the eternal Rock.*

—Isaiah 26:3-4 NLT

Journal Your Way to Significance

As a Christian, you received a new heart which gives you new abilities and attitudes. Your heart helps you desire and learn about God. Instead of being fearful, you can confidently love others with the power God provides.

Doubting your worth enables fear. Insecurity multiplies when you respond passively to difficult circumstances. When you fear, the ways you've not been perfected by love become obvious. God says you are not one who shrinks back in fear.

An active faith leads to strength, stability, and security. If you were a boat at sea, God would be your anchor. When the storms of life come, He will keep you from crashing into the rocks or capsizing in the waves. Ask God to increase your faith and trust in Him.

Truth #08

God Uses Truth To Strengthen You

[The devil] was a murderer from the beginning, and does not stand in the truth, because there is no truth in him. When he lies, he speaks out of his own character, for he is a liar and the father of lies.
—John 8:44 ESV

"Truly, truly, I say to you, he who does not enter the sheepfold by the door but climbs in by another way, that man is a thief and a robber. But he who enters by the door is the shepherd of the sheep. To him the gatekeeper opens. The sheep hear his voice, and he calls his own sheep by name and leads them out. When he has brought out all his own, he goes before them, and the sheep follow him, for they know his voice."
—John 10:1–4 ESV

The believer should assail the lies of the evil spirits. Every suggestion from the enemy must be met resolutely with the truth of the Bible. Answer doubts with faith; respond to despair with words of hope; reply to fear with words of peace. Open your heart to the Spirit's guidance. Victory is obtained by wielding the Sword of the Spirit.

—Watchman Nee (edited)

All Scripture is inspired by God and is useful to teach us what is true and to make us realize what is wrong in our lives. It corrects us when we are wrong and teaches us to do what is right. God uses it to prepare and equip his people to do every good work.

—2 Timothy 3:16-17 NLT

Journal Your Way to Significance

Jesus knows you intimately by your name. You aren't just another number. You're in God's family because He wants you there. Voices aligned with the devil speak lies meant to deceive and destroy. But lies only have power when you believe them and consider them to be true.

All voices are powerless to negate who you are. You are in control of how you choose to see yourself. You can discern Jesus's voice of truth and follow Him. With God on your side, you can recognize and ignore meaningless lies.

When you feel oppressed by thoughts that God isn't trustworthy or you aren't loveable expose those lies. Ask God to help you affirm His truth. God is trustworthy. Jesus is truth. The Holy Spirit says you are loved and significant.

Truth #09

God Uses Evil To Strengthen You

You must not eat from the tree of the knowledge of good and evil, for when you eat from it you will certainly die.

—Genesis 2:17 NIV

Afterward, the Holy Spirit led Jesus into the lonely wilderness in order to reveal his strength against the accuser by going through the ordeal of testing. And after fasting for forty days, Jesus was extremely weak and famished. Then the tempter came to entice him to provide food by doing a miracle. So he said to Jesus, "How can you possibly be the Son of God and go hungry? Just order these stones to be turned into loaves of bread." He answered, "The Scriptures say: Bread alone will not satisfy, but true life is found in every word, which constantly goes forth from God's mouth."

—Matthew 4:1-4 TPT

God's plan and purpose is to use Satan's temptations as a means of testing and strengthening our faith in Him. God allows tests in order that our spiritual "muscles" may be exercised and strengthened. Whether the testing is by God's initiative or by Satan's, God will always use it to produce good in us when we meet the test in His power.

—John MacArthur (edited)

No temptation has overtaken you that is not common to man. God is faithful, and he will not let you be tempted beyond your ability, but with the temptation he will also provide the way of escape, that you may be able to endure it.

—1 Corinthians 10:13 ESV

Journal Your Way to Significance

The fall of mankind into sin by eating from the tree of the knowledge of good and evil changed how the world works. If you want to grow stronger you must resist evil. This was impossible until God sent help.

The death and resurrection of Jesus changed the world again. He made the impossible, possible. Now, as you exercise self-control to overcome evil and the temptation to sin, you can learn how to show gentleness and kindness.

The more you doubt God, the weaker you will be. Sin is most tempting when your understanding of God and yourself are distorted. Because of Jesus you can change, "I'll take what I can get now because I doubt anything better is coming," to, "I trust God. My future is going to be awesome."

God Equips You With Power

You surely know that your body is a temple where the Holy Spirit lives. The Spirit is in you and is a gift from God.
—1 Corinthians 6:19 CEV

*For God gave us a spirit not of fear
but of power and love and self-control.*
—2 Timothy 1:7 ESV

[Jesus asked], "Do you believe in the Son of Man?" The man answered, "Who is he, sir? I want to believe in him." "You have seen him," Jesus said, "and he is speaking to you!" "Yes, Lord, I believe!" the man said. And he worshiped Jesus. Then Jesus told him, "I entered this world to render judgment—to give sight to the blind and to show those who think they see that they are blind."
—John 9:35-39 NLT

MATT PAVLIK

You cannot do God's work without God's power.
—John R. Rice

I tell you for certain that if you have faith in me, you will do the same things that I am doing. You will do even greater things, now that I am going back to the Father.
—John 14:12 CEV

Elisha prayed, "Open his eyes, Lord, so that he may see." Then the Lord opened the servant's eyes, and he looked and saw the hills full of horses and chariots of fire.
—2 Kings 6:17 NIV

Journal Your Way to Significance

You are significant because you are a temple for God's Spirit. No other creation has this honor. You're less than God but capable of doing greater works than Jesus. The Spirit equips and empowers you for new works—different than Jesus's.

Seeing from God's perspective is powerful. You gained your spiritual eyes the moment you believed in Jesus. Those who don't believe see with physical eyes, but are spiritually blind. That's not you! Look for God with your spiritual eyes.

Does it ever feel like God is unreachable, not present, or not listening? Try praying, "God, help me remember how to use my spiritual eyes." He will answer this kind of prayer. He said He'd never leave you. You and God are on the same team. You can walk confidently knowing God is with you.

You Are Savory

You are like salt for everyone on earth. But if salt no longer tastes like salt, how can it make food salty? All it is good for is to be thrown out and walked on.
—Matthew 5:13 CEV

Let your speech always be gracious, seasoned with salt, so that you may know how you ought to answer each person.
—Colossians 4:6 ESV

MATT PAVLIK

Any battle for victory, power, and deliverance - from ourselves and from sin - which is not based constantly upon the gazing and the beholding of the Lord Jesus, with the heart and life lifted up to Him, is doomed to failure.
—Alan Redpath

"I am the sprouting vine and you're my branches. As you live in union with me as your source, fruitfulness will stream from within you—but when you live separated from me you are powerless."
—John 15:5 TPT

Journal Your Way to Significance

Salt is an invaluable mineral that has multiple, unique purposes. It preserves food, softens water, alters freezing and boiling points, and sustains the body. There is no other natural resource like it.

When Jesus labels you "salt," He is teaching you about your identity. God made you to be valuable and useful. Because you have what others are missing, you are indispensable. A salt-without-savor identity would be bland, dull, and worthless.

Jesus says you're savory! He intends that you grow in awareness of who you are for the benefit of others. Your contributions add a unique flavor to others' experiences. Share God's salt, His truth and hope of eternal life, with others to preserve them. Help them see what is missing in their lives.

You Are Bright

You are like light for the whole world. A city built on top of a hill cannot be hidden, and no one would light a lamp and put it under a clay pot. A lamp is placed on a lampstand, where it can give light to everyone in the house. Make your light shine, so that others will see the good that you do and will praise your Father in heaven.

—Matthew 5:14–16 CEV

Rise up in splendor and be radiant, for your light has dawned, and Yahweh's glory now streams from you! Look carefully! Darkness blankets the earth, and thick gloom covers the nations, but Yahweh arises upon you and the brightness of his glory appears over you!

—Isaiah 60:1-2 TPT

MATT PAVLIK

To stand before the Holy One of eternity is to change. Resentments cannot be held with the same tenacity when we enter his gracious light.
—Richard J. Foster

Once your life was full of sin's darkness, but now you have the very light of our Lord shining through you because of your union with him. Your mission is to live as children flooded with his revelation-light! And the supernatural fruits of his light will be seen in you—goodness, righteousness, and truth.
—Ephesians 5:8-9 TPT

Journal Your Way to Significance

You couldn't survive without light. Light from the sun fights infection, provides warmth, and improves mood.

Jesus, The Light, illuminates who God is. Light has power to attract. When the light of Christ shines through you and reflects off of you, it creates a unique picture of who God is. Others need to see the image you can display.

A bright identity is helpful, beautiful, and worshipful. It is meant to be on display because it glorifies God. A shamefully hidden identity can't fully serve God's purposes. Jesus says you're bright! Evil is deceiving, destructive, and monotonous. There are a few ways to be evil, but there are infinite ways to be beautiful. Let your beauty shine before all. What is one aspect of your identity that the world needs today?

You Are Gifted

Now there are varieties of gifts, but the same Spirit; and there are varieties of service, but the same Lord; and there are varieties of activities, but it is the same God who empowers them all in everyone. To each is given the manifestation of the Spirit for the common good.

—1 Corinthians 12:4–7 ESV

Moses said to the people of Israel: The Lord has chosen Bezalel of the Judah tribe. Not only has the Lord filled him with his Spirit, but he has given him wisdom and made him a skilled craftsman who can create objects of art with gold, silver, bronze, stone, and wood.

—Exodus 35:30–33 CEV

MATT PAVLIK

Your greatest fulfillment in life will come when you discover your unique gifts and abilities and use them to edify others and glorify the LORD.
—Neil T. Anderson

As each has received a gift, use it to serve one another, as good stewards of God's varied grace: whoever speaks, as one who speaks oracles of God; whoever serves, as one who serves by the strength that God supplies—in order that in everything God may be glorified through Jesus Christ.
—1 Peter 4:10–11 ESV

Journal Your Way to Significance

God doesn't gift only a few people. He says, "to each is given"—meaning every believer is gifted. The purpose of whatever gift you have is to bless and strengthen the body of Christ.

God supplies what you need to serve others. There are a lot of needs, but God has ordained for you to serve according to your identity. You have a unique manifestation of God's Spirit. Because you declare who God is like no other person, you also serve like no other person.

God wants you to practice your spiritual gifting to increase your ability to support others. Your faith will grow as you experience the joy of God blessing others through you. Ask Jesus to reveal the depths of your spiritual gifting so that you can bless others.

You Are Needed

"Jeremiah, I am your Creator, and before you were born, I chose you to speak for me to the nations."
—Jeremiah 1:5 CEV

Then I heard the Lord asking, "Whom should I send as a messenger to this people? Who will go for us?" I said, "Here I am. Send me."
—Isaiah 6:8 NLT

MATT PAVLIK

View yourself as a precious vessel He crafted for a unique purpose.
—Patricia Ennis

But you are a chosen race, a royal priesthood, a holy nation, a people for his own possession, that you may proclaim the excellencies of him who called you out of darkness into his marvelous light.
—1 Peter 2:9 ESV

Journal Your Way to Significance

The creator of the universe doesn't need anyone, but He chose you to accomplish His plans. God isn't waiting for you to fail so He can fire you. You can work fearlessly to bring out what God placed in you and in others.

Because you are unique, you bring joy to God like no other. You belong in His family. No one else can draw others to Jesus in the same way you can. It is vitally important that you develop your potential to its fullest.

God chose you before you were born according to His sovereign plan. Your purpose is permanent; it has a past, a present, and a future. As long as you are on this earth, may you experience no doubt that God wants you to discover and fulfill your purpose. How will you respond to His call?

You Are Unique

For just as each of us has one body with many members, and these members do not all have the same function, so in Christ we, though many, form one body, and each member belongs to all the others. We have different gifts, according to the grace given to each of us.

—Romans 12:4–6 NIV

But God has put all parts of our body together in the way that he decided is best. A body isn't really a body, unless there is more than one part. It takes many parts to make a single body. That's why the eyes cannot say they don't need the hands. That's also why the head cannot say it doesn't need the feet. In fact, we cannot get along without the parts of the body that seem to be the weakest.

—1 Corinthians 12:18-22 CEV

MATT PAVLIK

The day that each person willingly accepts himself or herself for who he or she is and acknowledges their uniqueness of God's framing process marks the beginning of a journey to seeing the handiwork of God in each life.
—Ravi Zacharias

Before we were even born, he gave us our destiny; that we would fulfill the plan of God who always accomplishes every purpose and plan in his heart.
—Ephesians 1:11 TPT

Journal Your Way to Significance

God wants you to keep your identity and be like Christ. Let Jesus be the vine, your source of life. Let others be the branch that they are. They have their gifting, different than your ability. There's no competition to see who can be best at being you.

Accept that you are limited. You can't be the expert in every situation. But where you aren't gifted emphasizes all the more where you are gifted. Should a hammer worry about a screw that needs tightening? A hammer is made for nails. If it's beyond your purpose, it's not your responsibility.

Are you tired of being someone you aren't? Focus on exactly what God made you for. Leave the results to Him because He is all-wise and in control of all things. You will accomplish more of what is important.

You Are Enough

Be humble in the Lord's presence, and he will honor you.
—James 4:10 CEV

Another of his disciples, Andrew, Simon Peter's brother, spoke up, "Here is a boy with five small barley loaves and two small fish, but how far will they go among so many?" Jesus said, "Have the people sit down." There was plenty of grass in that place, and they sat down (about five thousand men were there). Jesus then took the loaves, gave thanks, and distributed to those who were seated as much as they wanted. He did the same with the fish. When they had all had enough to eat, he said to his disciples, "Gather the pieces that are left over. Let nothing be wasted."
—John 6:8–12 NIV

MATT PAVLIK

Jesus is the God whom we can approach without pride and before whom we can humble ourselves without despair.

—Blaise Pascal

Then Saul gave David his own armor—a bronze helmet and a coat of mail. David put it on, strapped the sword over it, and took a step or two to see what it was like, for he had never worn such things before. "I can't go in these," he protested to Saul. "I'm not used to them." So David took them off again. He picked up five smooth stones from a stream and put them into his shepherd's bag. Then, armed only with his shepherd's staff and sling, he started across the valley to fight the Philistine.

—1 Samuel 17:38-40 NLT

Journal Your Way to Significance

God is pleased with who you are, just as you are. Pretending to be someone you aren't doesn't help anyone. You can't go wrong if you remain true to who God made you to be. When you try to be someone else, you reject God's perfect design.

God wants all of you. Nothing more and nothing less. He doesn't care how much money or how many possessions you have. God wants you free from all that would hold you back from becoming all He intends you to be.

Don't underestimate what God can do with who you are. When you reach out in faith, you please God. God delights in you offering yourself to Him. He gives you the ability to choose to give. This makes your gift precious to Him. Offer who you are without striving to be any more or less.

Truth #17

You Are More Important Than Your Popularity

These all died in faith, not having received the things promised, but having seen them and greeted them from afar, and having acknowledged that they were strangers and exiles on the earth. For people who speak thus make it clear that they are seeking a homeland. ... they desire a better country, that is, a heavenly one. Therefore God is not ashamed to be called their God, for he has prepared for them a city.

—Hebrews 11:13–16 ESV

*Wise friends make you wise,
but you hurt yourself
by going around with fools.*

—Proverbs 13:20 CEV

MATT PAVLIK

If honest of heart and uprightness before God were lacking or if I did not patiently wait on God for instruction, or if I preferred the counsel of my fellow-men to the declarations of the Word of God, I made great mistakes.
—George Mueller

Many people did believe in him, however, including some of the Jewish leaders. But they wouldn't admit it for fear that the Pharisees would expel them from the synagogue. For they loved human praise more than the praise of God.
—John 12:42-43 NLT

Journal Your Way to Significance

You have value before you ever make a contribution. You belong even when you don't feel needed or wanted. Some years may pass while you continue to feel like you have no purpose. That's either because you're not ready for the world, or the world isn't ready for you.

The people of this world rejected Jesus, so they will also reject you. God has established you in heaven—your true home. God is proud to associate with you. You might not have any biological family on earth, but you have heavenly family.

Though you can't see your unique contribution... Though your efforts appear to fall on deaf ears... Though multitudes are indifferent to your presence... Though the world may reject you... you still have a heavenly home where you belong.

Truth #18

You Are More Important Than Your Possessions

Better to be poor and honest than to be dishonest and rich.
—Proverbs 28:6 NLT

Yet true godliness with contentment is itself great wealth. After all, we brought nothing with us when we came into the world, and we can't take anything with us when we leave it. So if we have enough food and clothing, let us be content. But people who long to be rich fall into temptation and are trapped by many foolish and harmful desires that plunge them into ruin and destruction. For the love of money is the root of all kinds of evil. And some people, craving money, have wandered from the true faith and pierced themselves with many sorrows.
—1 Timothy 6:6-10 NLT

MATT PAVLIK

Do not let your happiness depend on something you may lose. If love is to be a blessing, not a misery, it must be for the only Beloved who will never pass away.
—C.S. Lewis, The Four Loves

What will you gain, if you own the whole world but destroy yourself or waste your life?
—Luke 9:25 CEV

Journal Your Way to Significance

What if the emotional and spiritual state you are in when you die is the one you must remain in for eternity? Does that motivate you to spend more time maturing? Possessions eventually become boring. Growth lasts forever.

Accumulating wealth should never be your primary goal. It is a means to an end, not an end in itself. When you try to make it an end, it becomes a dead end. Possessions might initially impress others, but the only way to influence others for lasting change is to invest in becoming more like Jesus.

When you are in touch with your true worth, then you should be free from deep cravings to be rich. There is no greater high than functioning in the capacity that God intends for you. What kingdom purpose gives you a natural high?

Truth #19

You Are More Important Than Your Performance

But he replied, "My kindness is all you need. My power is strongest when you are weak." So if Christ keeps giving me his power, I will gladly brag about how weak I am. Yes, I am glad to be weak or insulted or mistreated or to have troubles and sufferings, if it is for Christ. Because when I am weak, I am strong.
—2 Corinthians 12:9-10 CEV

For God is working in you, giving you the desire and the power to do what pleases him.
—Philippians 2:13 NLT

MATT PAVLIK

If you do base your life on how many touchdowns you score, how many championships you win, then when you have a setback, then when you have an injury, you're not playing, or something goes wrong, your self-worth goes down.
—Tim Tebow

When you eat or drink or do anything else, always do it to honor God.
—1 Corinthians 10:31 CEV

Journal Your Way to Significance

Paul figured out how to live in the zone. Whatever he did, he aimed to honor God. Because he could fully rely on God's grace, he didn't need to care how life treated him. He knew his motives were right if all he did was for Christ.

God wants you to give your all to the tasks before you, then leave the results up to Him. You can't earn your worth. You can only receive it independent of whatever you accomplish.

Attempting to earn your worth through performance is like running on a treadmill. It's a lot of effort, but you never get anywhere. You'll need to outperform yourself every time to continue to receive praise—and it won't be enough to fill the hole in your soul. Only God's endless supply of love can fill your self-worth. It will take you farther then you can imagine.

Truth #20

You Are More Important Than Your Pride

Do you want to be a mighty warrior?
It's better to be known as one
who is patient and slow to anger.
Do you want to conquer a city?
Rule over your temper before
you attempt to rule a city.
—Proverbs 16:32 TPT

If you walk with the mockers you will learn to mock,
but God's grace and favor flow to the meek.
—Proverbs 3:33-34 TPT

Anybody can become angry - that is easy, but to be angry with the right person and to the right degree and at the right time and for the right purpose, and in the right way - that is not within everybody's power and is not easy.

—Aristotle

But now you must put them all away: anger, wrath, malice, slander, and obscene talk from your mouth. Do not lie to one another, seeing that you have put off the old self with its practices and have put on the new self, which is being renewed in knowledge after the image of its creator.

—Colossians 3:8-10 ESV

Journal Your Way to Significance

Many people deny their anger, sadness, or fear. This only delays (at best) or prevents (at worst) a resolution to the problem. Consequences for denying your feelings range from physical symptoms such as headaches and ulcers to serious emotional symptoms such as depression and panic.

Anger likely indicates that you feel like your significance is threatened. Only God has perfectly righteous anger. So you must train yourself to rule over your temper.

You must learn to express your anger in non-destructive ways. Before you act on your anger, identify why are you angry. Then, be sure to enlist God's help in using your anger for constructive purposes. How angry are you? In what ways do you feel threatened? What restitution do you need?

Truth #21

Your Faith Nourishes Your Self-Worth

This Good News tells us how God makes us right in his sight. This is accomplished from start to finish by faith. As the Scriptures say, "It is through faith that a righteous person has life."

—Romans 1:17 NLT

Now faith brings our hopes into reality and becomes the foundation needed to acquire the things we long for. It is all the evidence required to prove what is still unseen. And without faith living within us it would be impossible to please God. For we come to God in faith knowing that he is real and that he rewards the faith of those who give all their passion and strength into seeking him.

—Hebrews 11:1, 6 TPT

MATT PAVLIK

Humility is to make a right estimate of one's self.
—Charles Spurgeon

Humility is truth.
—Desiderius Erasmus

For by the grace given to me I say to everyone among you not to think of himself more highly than he ought to think, but to think with sober judgment, each according to the measure of faith that God has assigned.
—Romans 12:3 ESV

Journal Your Way to Significance

Faith allows you to see your true potential so use it to evaluate your worth. Look at yourself through God's loving eyes. You can reach perfection by allowing God to transform you into all He has made you to be. When considering your ability, be neither self-deprecating nor arrogant. Be honest.

Healthy comparison should not negatively impact anyone's worth. Comparison is only beneficial for seeing how rare and valuable everybody is in the Body of Christ.

God wants you to be all you can be by using all He has given you without trying to be everything to everybody. Focus on the race God has set before you. Your start and finish lines are different than others'. You are competing against yourself. You can cheer others on in the events they are running.

God Made You For Peace And Contentment

Even so, I have noticed one thing, at least, that is good. It is good for people to eat, drink, and enjoy their work under the sun during the short life God has given them, and to accept their lot in life. And it is a good thing to receive wealth from God and the good health to enjoy it. To enjoy your work and accept your lot in life—this is indeed a gift from God. God keeps such people so busy enjoying life that they take no time to brood over the past.

—Ecclesiastes 5:18-20 NLT

For the kingdom of God is not a matter of eating and drinking but of righteousness and peace and joy in the Holy Spirit.

—Romans 14:17 ESV

MATT PAVLIK

God can't give us peace and happiness apart from Himself because there is no such thing.

—C.S. Lewis

*Don't be annoyed by anyone who does wrong,
and don't envy them.
Do what the LORD wants,
and he will give you your heart's desire.
Be patient and trust the LORD.
Don't let it bother you when all goes well
for those who do sinful things.
Don't be angry or furious.
Anger can lead to sin.*

—Psalm 37:1,4,7,8 CEV

Journal Your Way to Significance

Peace and joy are possible because Jesus declared you righteous. The Holy Spirit manifests peace and joy in your life as you align yourself with God's way of thinking. You'll never go unfulfilled when you're living out who God made you to be. Who God is and who you are, are enough to fill you.

You can't feel important and irritated at the same time. You can't realize your significance when you are busy worrying. Circumstances provide the opportunity for you to discover your true identity. They reveal your potential.

God doesn't take back His gifts of identity and salvation; they are permanently yours. Since you are free, pursue God's heart instead of things like fame or fortune. Ask God to help you see His way of thinking so you will have peace and joy.

Truth #23

God Made You To Experience Abundant Life Forever

The thief's purpose is to steal and kill and destroy. My purpose is to give them a rich and satisfying life.

—John 10:10 NLT

But there is more! Now that God has accepted us because Christ sacrificed his life's blood, we will also be kept safe from God's anger. Even when we were God's enemies, he made peace with us, because his Son died for us. Yet something even greater than friendship is ours. Now that we are at peace with God, we will be saved by his Son's life.

—Romans 5:9-10 CEV

What were we made for? To know God. What aim should we have in life? To know God. What is the eternal life that Jesus gives? To know God. What is the best thing in life? To know God. What in humans gives God most pleasure? Knowledge of himself.
—J. I. Packer

Eternal life means to know and experience you as the only true God, and to know and experience Jesus Christ, as the Son whom you have sent.
—John 17:3 TPT

Journal Your Way to Significance

God made you to live forever, which is awesome. But how happy are you today? Would you want to live forever in your current condition? Living forever is different than possessing eternal life. Having eternal life means you have access to the highest quality of life possible today.

The more you know Jesus, the more enjoyable your life will be. Once you belong to God, He renews your spirit so you'll last forever. Jesus lives in you, working to help you perform at your highest level of functioning.

Possessing eternal life should influence your daily choices. You can risk because you can't lose anything important. Every good deed you do counts for something in God's economy. What do you need to do to make the most of your eternal life?

Truth #24

Your Words Are Meaningful

*Sharing words of wisdom
is satisfying to your inner being.
It encourages you to know that
you've changed someone else's life.
Your words are so powerful that
they will kill or give life, and
the talkative person will
reap the consequences.*
—Proverbs 18:20-21 TPT

*Timely advice is lovely,
like golden apples in a silver basket.*
—Proverbs 25:11 NLT

MATT PAVLIK

*Kind words can be short and easy to speak,
but their echoes are truly endless.*
—Mother Teresa

*May the words of my mouth
and the meditation of my heart
be pleasing to you,
O LORD, my rock and my redeemer.*
—Psalm 19:14 NLT

Journal Your Way to Significance

God's words are significant. You're made in His image, so your words are too. Words have power to change the world. Words reveal the condition of the speaker's heart.

Jesus is the Word made flesh. The combination of His humanness and deity helps us understand God. Just like Jesus makes it easier to understand God, your words make it easier for others to understand who you are.

When God created you, He made you open to the spoken word. Words can build you up or tear you down. Words have the power to kill or give life. Words spoken against God's truth have no roots in reality. They will wither and die. Recognize and reject them, especially when you are the one about to speak. How well do your words communicate truth and life?

Your Actions Are Meaningful

What good is it, my brothers, if someone says he has faith but does not have works? Can that faith save him? If a brother or sister is poorly clothed and lacking in daily food, and one of you says to them, "Go in peace, be warmed and filled," without giving them the things needed for the body, what good is that? So also faith by itself, if it does not have works, is dead.

—James 2:14-17 ESV

So whoever knows the right thing to do and fails to do it, for him it is sin.

—James 4:17 ESV

MATT PAVLIK

People who use time wisely spend it on activities that advance their overall purpose in life.
—John C. Maxwell

And may the Lord our God show us his approval and make our efforts successful. Yes, make our efforts successful!
—Psalm 90:17 NLT

Journal Your Way to Significance

You have a choice with what you will do with your life. You have the ability to act intentionally just like God does. You make a difference by what you do and don't do.

Depression and anxiety prevent you from being who God made you to be. They distract you from seeing God's goodness. Fearful and gloomy thoughts consume the energy meant to serve God. The worse you feel, the more essential it is for you to act intentionally. Be ready to receive as much help as you need so you can function at your best.

Being a positive presence is enough to make a difference. If you become discouraged, doubt, and stop trying to make a difference, there will be a loss. The world needs to hear all about your God experiences—how He is working in your life.

You Have A Destiny To Fulfill

A person's steps are directed by the LORD.
How then can anyone understand their own way?
—Proverbs 20:24 NIV

For we are his workmanship, created in Christ Jesus for good works, which God prepared beforehand, that we should walk in them.
—Ephesians 2:10 ESV

MATT PAVLIK

Our greatest fear should not be of failure but of succeeding at things in life that don't really matter.
—Francis Chan

You keep every promise you've ever made to me! Since your love for me is constant and endless, I ask you, Lord, to finish every good thing that you've begun in me!
—Psalm 138:8 TPT

Journal Your Way to Significance

God wants you to pursue His purposes for creating you. No one can cancel God's will. Your identity is who you are. Your destiny is where you are going. Your circumstances don't determine your identity or your destiny.

God is in control and He defines success. Losing never feels good but it need not be your concern. Your destiny is secured by your union with Christ. You might not understand why God allowed you to lose a particular battle, but you are a winner because God's purposes will prevail in the end.

Nothing can stop God's vision for your life. He created you with just the right identity for the good works He has in mind. Welcome the adventure to discover all God made you to be and all He has planned for you. That's your legacy.

You Are Unstoppable

*Weapons made to attack you
won't be successful;
words spoken against you
won't hurt at all.
my servants, Jerusalem is yours!
I, the LORD, promise
to bless you with victory.*
—Isaiah 54:17 CEV

*In everything we have won more than a victory
because of Christ who loves us.*
—Romans 8:37 CEV

MATT PAVLIK

God means every Christian to be effective, to make a difference in the actual records and results of Christian work. God put each of us here to be a power. There is not one of us but is an essential wheel of the machinery and can accomplish all that God calls us to.

—A. B. Simpson

A person may have many ideas concerning God's plan for his life, but only the designs of his purpose will succeed in the end.

—Proverbs 19:21 TPT

Journal Your Way to Significance

As you journey through life, at times you'll feel the enemy's breath on your neck. The enemy relentlessly pursues you, intent upon destroying you, but God's Spirit is faster and stronger. Even when it seems like God's plans are failing, He always has another play that allows His purpose to prevail.

You are inseparably bound to Jesus's victory. Jesus overcame death and is glorified, so you will be too. You're unstoppable because God is unstoppable. There is no reason to stop until God says it is your time to stop.

Who is greater than the Lord? God fuels you with abundance, peace, and power. You are more than alive; you can meet every challenge in triumph. You will accomplish every good work that God has planned for your life.

Death Is A Doorway

Let me make this clear: A single grain of wheat will never be more than a single grain of wheat unless it drops into the ground and dies. Because then it sprouts and produces a great harvest of wheat—all because one grain died. "The person who loves his life and pampers himself will miss true life! But the one who detaches his life from this world and abandons himself to me, will find true life and enjoy it forever!

—John 12:24-25 TPT

Now when David had served God's purpose in his own generation, he fell asleep; he was buried with his ancestors and his body decayed.

—Acts 13:36 NIV

MATT PAVLIK

*If a man hasn't discovered something that
he will die for, he isn't fit to live.*
—Martin Luther King Jr.

*And everyone who lives because of faith in me
will never really die. Do you believe this?"*
—John 11:26 CEV

Journal Your Way to Significance

Your life on earth isn't over until you have served God's purpose. For the believer, death is like a second birthday or a job promotion. When you fear death, you rob yourself of the best life you can have today.

Life is a bitter-sweet squeeze between enjoying all that life has to offer and sacrificing momentary pleasure for eternal gain. The more you resist the journey, the slower time seems to pass. But when you enjoy the journey, time flies by.

If someone could see your life, what would they conclude is most important to you? Have a heart-to-heart with God about your priorities. What matters more to you than your life? What adjustments might help you find the sweet-spot of enjoyment no matter your circumstances?

Truth #29

Your Sacrifice Is Substantial

Do not neglect to do good and to share what you have, for such sacrifices are pleasing to God.
—Hebrews 13:16 ESV

Dear friends, God is good. So I beg you to offer your bodies to him as a living sacrifice, pure and pleasing. That's the most sensible way to serve God.
—Romans 12:1 CEV

We do this by keeping our eyes on Jesus, the champion who initiates and perfects our faith. Because of the joy awaiting him, he endured the cross, disregarding its shame. Now he is seated in the place of honor beside God's throne.
—Hebrews 12:2 NLT

MATT PAVLIK

You never hear Jesus say in Pilate's judgement hall one word that would let you imagine that He was sorry that He had undertaken so costly a sacrifice for us. When His hands are pierced, when He is parched with fever, His tongue dried up like a shard of pottery, when His whole body is dissolved into the dust of death, you never hear a groan or a shriek that looks like Jesus is going back on His commitment.

—Charles Spurgeon

*Greater love has no one than this,
that someone lay down his life for his friends.*

—John 15:13 ESV

Jesus refused to dull His senses during His crucifixion. He chose to experience the pain of His sacrifice. But He also felt joy as He laid down His life, knowing it was His Father's plan.

Immediately after Jesus's death, His followers thought He was gone forever. They lacked the faith to understand until they saw Him resurrected. At first, a genuine sacrifice will seem like the wrong idea. So, it must be done by faith, without avoiding the pain or grumbling about it.

If God asked you to give up what you consider important for the greater good, could you do it? Would you do it? Sacrifice will cost you, but it's always worth it. Having confidence that it is worth it and following Jesus's example in His sacrifice, you will also reap the same joy.

You Have A Mission To Fulfill

How can people have faith in the Lord and ask him to save them, if they have never heard about him? And how can they hear, unless someone tells them? And how can anyone tell them without being sent by the Lord? The Scriptures say it is a beautiful sight to see even the feet of someone coming to preach the good news.

—Romans 10:14-15 CEV

The kingdom of heaven is like what happens when a shop owner is looking for fine pearls. After finding a very valuable one, the owner goes and sells everything in order to buy that pearl.

—Matthew 13:45-46 CEV

MATT PAVLIK

Many persons have a wrong idea of what constitutes true happiness. It is not attained through self-gratification but through fidelity to a worthy purpose.
—Helen Keller

Jesus came and told his disciples, "I have been given all authority in heaven and on earth. Therefore, go and make disciples of all the nations, baptizing them in the name of the Father and the Son and the Holy Spirit. Teach these new disciples to obey all the commands I have given you. And be sure of this: I am with you always, even to the end of the age."
—Matthew 28:18-20 NLT

Journal Your Way to Significance

The ultimate satisfaction comes when you surrender your life to a cause greater than yourself. Enjoying this life only becomes wrong if it comes at the expense of God's real mission. Everything you do should in some way align with who God is, who you are, and furthering God's kingdom.

Remember, there is more to life which you cannot yet see. Don't stop short of overcoming the obstacles in your way. Stay focused on exploring and expanding God's kingdom. If you do these things, your heart will overflow with satisfaction as you behold the beauty of God's kingdom.

God placed a one of a kind significance within you that will burst forth as you focus on furthering God's kingdom. You will accomplish a unique work that He created only for you.

JOURNAL IN LAYERS

Now that you have completed the first pass through these truths, remember to revisit the them and your writing to gain the full benefit. You might be amazed at what you understood at first. But you can learn more with each pass you make.

To gain the most from journaling, here are some other journal-in-layers techniques to try:

- Return at a regular interval to followup with your previous entry. This is the secret to developing deeper truth in your heart.
- Limit the number of truths you explore in each layer. For example, focus on the first seven truths in a week. Revisit them each week for four weeks. Or, if God is speaking to you through one particular truth, focus on it for several days.
- Focus on only one scripture at a time. Review one verse from each lesson, then journal another layer.
- Focus on the lesson's quote or picture.
- Draw your own picture that represents the truth.
- Write your own prayer in response to the lesson.
- Focus on one particular emotion you feel as you read the lesson. Write about that feeling and other times you've felt that way.
- Focus on the past if you need healing. Focus on the present if you feel anxious. Focus on the future if you feel restless.

Have you tried another technique that works for you? Would you like to share how has this book been a blessing to you? Contact me at mpavlik@christianconcepts.com. You can learn more about journaling by getting *Soar Like Eagles* at ChristianConcepts.com.

ABOUT MATT PAVLIK

Matt Pavlik is a licensed professional clinical counselor who wants each individual restored to their true identity. He completed his Masters in Clinical Pastoral Counseling from Ashland Theological Seminary and his Bachelors in Computer Science from the University of Illinois.

He's been a Christian since 1991 and started journaling around that time. Matt and his wife Georgette have been married since 1999 and live with their four children in Centerville, Ohio.

Blogger

Learn more at ChristianConcepts.com.

Professional Counselor

Matt has more than 15 years of experience counseling individuals and couples at his Christian private practice, New Reflections Counseling (NewReflectionsCounseling.com).

Author

Matt has written over five books on Christian identity, marriage, and spiritual life. Visit ChristianConcepts.com, ToIdentityAndBeyond.com, ConfidentIdentity.com, and MarriageFromRootsToFruits.com for details.

Identity and Marriage Books

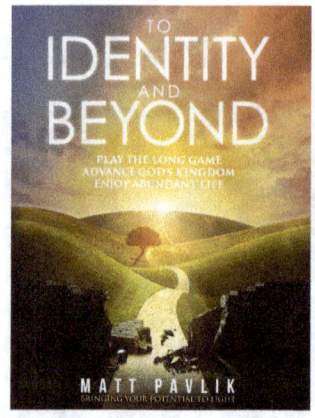  

Journal Your Way Books

Coming Soon

If you like *Journal Your Way To Significance*, you'll love these other titles:
- Journal Your Way To Love
- Journal Your Way To Security
- Journal Your Way To Connection

www.ingramcontent.com/pod-product-compliance
Lightning Source LLC
Chambersburg PA
CBHW050408130526
44592CB00047B/1454